# UkrainianLessons.com

**GET COMPLIMENTARY AUDIO TRACKS AT:**
ukrainianlessons.com/audiobook2973

Natalia Pendiur, Anna Ohoiko

# Ukrainian Handwriting Book

A progressive approach to learning to write Ukrainian in cursive
Created specifically for learners of Ukrainian as a foreign language
Includes pronunciation guidelines and audio recordings

Ukrainian Lessons
2022

Copyright © 2022 Ukrainian Lessons / Natalia Pendiur (Наталія Пендюр) / Anna Ohoiko (Анна Огойко)

All rights reserved. No part of this publication may be reproduced, stored in a retrieval system, or transmitted in any form or by any means, electronic, mechanical, photocopying, recording, or otherwise, without the prior written permission of the publisher.

Cover design: Oleksandra Siryk (Олександра Сірик)
Book interior design: Oleksandr Mashlai (Олександр Машлай), Oleksandra Siryk (Олександра Сірик)
Illustrations: Natalia Pendiur (Наталія Пендюр)
Production editor: Anna Ohoiko (Анна Огойко)
Copy editors: Kateryna Smuk (Катерина Смук), Kiana Smith
Assistant: Maryna Serbyna (Марина Сербина)

**Abstract:**
Whether you are just starting out to learn Ukrainian or want to finally learn how to write in cursive Cyrillic, this colorful workbook will be your guide.

It is designed specifically for Ukrainian language learners to learn how to write by hand in Ukrainian, develop a better understanding of texts written in Cyrillic, and improve reading and pronunciation skills.

While colorful illustrations and fun exercises will bring joy to your learning experience, the gradual thought-through approach (from the most common letters to more complicated and less common ones) will motivate you to keep going.

From a single letter to syllables, words, and short texts — master your Cyrillic handwriting and enjoy learning Ukrainian with this delightful workbook!

**Publisher Contact Information**
Anna Ohoiko
anna@ukrainianlessons.com
ukrainianlessons.com

ISBN: 978-91-986937-6-8

# Table of Contents

# Index of letters

### Why should you learn how to handwrite in Ukrainian?

If you are an owner of this book, you might have already answered this question. (And you are also a true **молодець** — good girl or boy for going for it!). Here are some more reasons why learning Ukrainian handwriting is useful and fun:

- **By practicing handwriting, you will expand different Ukrainian skills.** This book will help you get immersed in the language in a very special way — by writing its beautiful letters in cursive. At the same time, you will encounter new words and get used to some aspects of grammar, like endings and forms of the words. Letter by letter, you will build your confidence as a language learner.

- **If you regularly write in Ukrainian, you will learn more effectively.** Clicking on the screen or making notes electronically is usually a less effective way to learn a language. In our book, you will have plenty of space to practice writing and play with the language — which will allow you to continue studying using a pen and paper and learn more quickly.

- **You will learn not only how to write but also how to read cursive Ukrainian.** Just compare how different printed letters look versus cursive ones (especially **т, д, г**):

Перейти гори буде нелегко.

*Перейти гори буде нелегко.*

If you have been to Ukraine, you must have noticed that handwritten or cursive Ukrainian is everywhere — on ads and announcements, in doctor's prescriptions, or in personal notes. So even if you don't want to learn how to write, being able to read handwritten Ukrainian is essential.

- **You will greatly impress others.** If you have a Ukrainian sweetheart, Valentine's card, handwritten by you, will melt his or her heart. Plus, you can brag about your super skills to anyone.

- **You will keep your brain healthy.** Scientists who study the human brain talk about handwriting as a part of graphomotor skills. If those skills are not trained, functions of the brain that perceive language can also be underdeveloped. Anyone who does not write by hand is emotionally immature because certain interactions in the brain do not occur. By developing your writing skills, you keep your brain in good shape.

## How to work with this book?

1. I recommend that you go through the pages of this book **in order**, which is not alphabetical — it starts with **O** and moves through the most common and easy letters to the less frequent and more difficult ones.
   Each time you start a new letter, its chapter will include examples with letters that were already taught. I created and tested this system with my students, and it proved to be very effective.

2. Have a look at the **uppercase** and **lowercase** letters in **printed** and **cursive**. Compare them.

3. Read a short introduction about **pronunciation** written by my colleague Anna. Listen to the accompanying audio recorded by her to get used to hearing the sounds correctly. You can get access to the audio tracks at: ukrainianlessons.com/audiobook2973

4. Start practicing by writing a **letter by itself** — follow the sequence and direction of arrows. These handwriting guidelines are the ones used in Ukrainian schools.

5. After a single letter, move to **syllables**. Pay special attention to the ways the letter is linked with the previous or next letter — these junctions are often the hardest to master. Try to copy our examples — they are the correct and most used ones.

6. Gradually move to **words** and then **phrases**. There is space for your writing and, if you want to practice more, we have extra sheets at the end of the book.

7. There are also some **exercises** included — they might entertain you in the middle of monotonous handwriting work and teach you something new. You don't need to know any extra words or grammar to do them. In fact, some rules are briefly explained with examples for you.

8. Try to also listen to the **audio** when you can (link in step #3). At Ukrainian Lessons, we want to give you the opportunity to listen to the language as much as possible. Without sound, you might think in your head that the word or phrase is pronounced one way, but in fact, it is slightly different. Our complimentary audio will help you tackle pronunciation and develop your writing skills at the same time.

I have never written, as we say in Ukrainian, **каліграфічно** — calligraphically. My first teacher at school used to say, "What a wonderful day! Even Natalia's handwriting is not so bad." I had a hard time making the captions for illustrations in this book — they always came out crooked.

However, I have been jotting down quick thoughts and notes by hand for many years. I don't think you have to write like a master of calligraphy — unless you want to. But the ability to write by hand will definitely make you more confident in your language skills. Just imagine how proud you would be of yourself after completing this whole workbook.

Because what if someone gave you a love note or an important shopping list in Ukrainian? Or what if you found a message in a bottle in the Black Sea? Or a letter from your Ukrainian ancestors?

So get your pen or pencil... **До роботи!** — Let's get to work!

Natalia Pendiur
Ukrainian teacher, writer, and artist

# Українська абетка

| | | | | |
|---|---|---|---|---|
| А а /a/ | Б б /be/ | В в /ve/ | Г г /he/ | Ґ ґ /ge/ |
| Д д /de/ | Е е /e/ | Є є /je/ | Ж ж /zhe/ | З з /ze/ |
| И и /y (ı)/ | І і /i/ | Ї ї /ji/ | Й й /jot/ | К к /ka/ |
| Л л /el/ | М м /em/ | Н н /en/ | О о /o/ | П п /pe/ |
| Р р /er/ | С с /es/ | Т т /te/ | У у /u/ | Ф ф /ef/ |
| Х х /kha/ | Ц ц /tse/ | Ч ч /che/ | Ш ш /sha/ | Щ щ /shcha/ |
| ь /mjakyj znak/ | Ю ю /ju/ | Я я /ja/ | | |

# Українська абетка

А а   Б б   В в   Г г   Ґ ґ

Д д   Е е   Є є   Ж ж   З з

И и   І і   Ї ї   Й й   К к

Л л   М м   Н н   О о   П п

Р р   С с   Т т   У у   Ф ф

Х х   Ц ц   Ч ч   Ш ш   Щ щ

ь   Ю ю   Я я

## /O/ — LIKE O IN PORT

**Oro!** Wow! Although the Ukrainian **O** looks just like the English **O**, it doesn't sound exactly like the **o** in *office, brother,* or *alone*. We find it much closer to the first sound in ***au*thor**.

O O O O O

O O O O O O

O O O O O O O O O O O O O O O O O O O O O O

O O O O O O O O O O O O O O O

Find and underline "o" in the sentence below. Then write on top of the grey words to try what Ukrainian cursive feels like.

*Оксана, Оля і Соломія у школі*

Oksana, Olya and Solomiya are at the school

*іноземних мов.*

of foreign languages.

*Оксана, Оля і Соломія у школі*

*іноземних мов.*

One can express different emotions with "o":

# К к

## /КА/ — LIKE К IN КEY

К is one of those letters you love because it sounds almost exactly like /k/ in English. Take a notice: lowercase Ukrainian к doesn't have a long line like the English *k*.

К К

к к

*К К К К К К К К К*

*к к к к к к к к к*

*Ко Ко Ко Ко Ко Ко Ко Ко Ко*

*Ко Ко Ко Ко Ко Ко Ко Ко Ко*

*Око Око Око Око Око*

око

*Око Око Око Око*

eye

Even though it's not in Ukrainian dictionaries yet, sometimes we write the word ОК (okay). Try to do it too!

*ОК Ок Ок Ок Ок Ок*

ок

*Ок Ок Ок Ок Ок*

# I i

## /I/ — LIKE EE IN MEET

Ukrainian **i** is pronounced like the English *ee* (sw**ee**t). It is a very useful word by itself: **i** means "and" in Ukrainian.

I I

i i

*J J J J J J J J J J J J*

*i i i i i i i i i i i i*

*Iк Iк Iк Iк Iк Iо Iо Iо Iо*

*кi кi кi кi кi iк iк iк iк*

Find and underline **i, к, о**:

Колискова

Lullaby

Котику сіренький, котику біленький,

Little gray cat, little white cat,

Котку волохатий, не ходи по хаті.

Little hairy cat, don't walk around the house.

# T T

**/TE/ — LIKE T IN STOP**

Ukrainian **T** is pronounced similarly to the English /t/, but there is less air coming out with it — it is more gentle.

T T

T T

Тт Тт Тт Тт Тт Тт Тт Тт Тт

т т т т т т т т т т

Ти Ти Ти Ти Ти Ти Ти *Those*

То То То То То То То *That*

ти ти ти ти ти ти ти ти ти *those*

то то то то то то то то то *that*

от от от от от от *here*

оти оти оти оти *those*

кіт кіт кіт кіт кіт *cat*

кіт

18

# A a

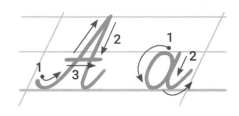

## /A/ — LIKE A IN START

**A** is the first letter of the Ukrainian alphabet and it is easy to pronounce. Open your mouth /waɪd/ when saying Ukrainian **A**!

A A

a a

*А А*

*а а*

*Ам Ам*

*Ак Ак*

*ка ка*

*ма ма*

that (feminine gender)

*так так*

yes

*мік-мак мік-мак*

tick-tock

*мік-мак!*

# E e

## /E/ — LIKE E IN TEST

E sounds roughly like the /e/ in the English words p**e**t, b**e**d, or the first sound in **e**nergy. However, when **E** is not stressed, it is weaker and it sounds a little closer to **И**.

E E

e e

*Ɛ Ɛ*

*e e*

*Ɛк Ɛк*

*Ɛm Ɛm*

*ea ea*

E-e-e is a filler sound

*ке ке*

*me me*

that (neuter gender)

*маке маке*

such / so (neuter gender)

20

# P p

## /ER/ — CLOSE TO R IN RUG

Here is a tough one! **P** is not /p/ in /p/roblem, but rather the /r/ in it. Actually, it is quite different from /r/, it is a "rolled r". You might need to train your muscles to get it right, check out Ukrainian Lessons Podcast — Episode #25 for some tips and practice!

P P

p p

*P P*

*p p*

*Pi Pi*      *Pa Pa*

*op op*      *ep ep*

*pi pi*

*pe pe*

*pa pa*

*mp mp*

рік рік

ріка ріка

рак рак

кора кора

кріт кріт

карта карта

Карта

Change cursive to print:

Коротко

Change print to cursive:

# Ракета

 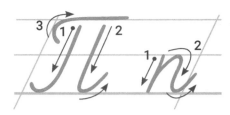

## /PE/ — LIKE P IN PARK

**П** — це не **П**роблема. **П** is not a *Problem*. It is pronounced like /p/ in English, but in Ukrainian you put less pressure on your lips, do it softer.

П П

П П

*П П*

*п п*

*Пі Пі*      *Пр Пр*

*па па*      *про про*      about

*пе пе*      *пт пт*

*еп еп*

*ап ап*

You might know the mathematical constant — $\pi$ — pi — 3,1415927... In Ukrainian it is **пі**:

*пі пі*

*пара пара*
                        steam, couple

*парк парк*
                        park

*Кіпр Кіпр*
                        Cyprus

*Кіпр*

*Петро Петро*
                        Petro (male name)

*портрет портрет*
                        portrait

*портрет Петра*
                        portrait of Petro

*портрет Петра*

Match the words with the pictures. Then change cursive to print.

*рок* ☐      *Поттер* ☐      *парк* ☐

*1*

*2*

*3*

# C c

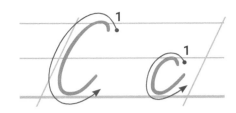

## /ES/ — LIKE S IN STOP

Here's a secret — **секрет**. **C** in Ukrainian is always pronounced as its name in the English alphabet (/si/ — /s/).

C C

C C

C C

c c

Ce Ce

Ca Ca

ce ce

ca ca

ci ci          cm cm

ac ac          ic ic

сто сто

hundred

пес пес

dog

оса оса

wasp

сік сік

juice

каса каса

checkout/

коса коса

braid

коса

краса краса

beauty

паспорт паспорт

passport

кіт Кріс і пес Петро

cat Chris and dog Petro

кіт Кріс і пес Петро

# И и

## /Y (I)/ — CLOSE TO I IN DID

Compare the **И** sound to the short /ɪ/ in the English words *a bit, a little*. Ukrainian **И** is similar, but a little longer and deeper. Pronunciation of **И** can be quite challenging for Ukrainian learners. Check out Ukrainian Lessons Podcast — Episode #5 to learn some tricks and get practice!

И И

и и

И И

и и

ри ри       ки ки

ни ни       ии ии

ии ии       ис ис

ир ир       ти ти

you (singular)

сир сир

cheese

рис рис

rice

*кіт кіт*

cat

*кит кит*

whale

*скрипка скрипка*

violin

By adding **-и** to some nouns you get plural forms. Make plural nouns by adding **-и** to the models:

*сир — сири*

cheese — cheeses

*коса — коси*

braid — braids

*кит — кит_*

whale — whales

*карта — карт_*

map — maps

*парк — парк_*

park — parks

*паспорт — паспорт_*

passport — passports

*ракета — ракет_*

rocket — rockets

Fill in with appropriate letters. You must have seen these words before!

*к_т*       *к_т*

# B B

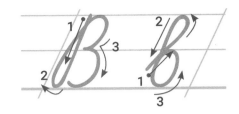

## /VE/ — LIKE V IN VAN

At first, you might confuse it with **Б** (**Б**анан — Banana)... But with some practice you will get used to **B** pronounced as the first sound in **B**ідео — *Video*.

B B

B B

*B B*

*в в*

*Bе Bе*        *Bі Bі*

*ів ів*        *ев ев*

*ви ви*

you (plural)

*ві ві*

Now you can write "Hi!" in Ukrainian! 🎉

*Привіт! Привіт!*

віра віра

faith

Віра Віра

Vira (female name)

квітка квітка

flower

Квітка красива. Квітка красива.

The flower is beautiful.

кава кава

coffee

кава

— Привіт, Петре!

— Hello, Petro!

— Привіт, Пітере!

— Hello, Peter!

— Кави?

— Coffee?

— Так!

— Yes!

# Б б

 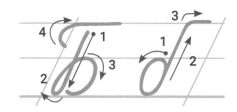

## /BE/ — LIKE B IN BEST

It may look unfamiliar, but **Б** has equivalents in many languages. In English, it sounds like /b/ in **B**anana.

Б Б

Б Б

Б Б

б б

Бр Бр      Бе Бе

бо бо

because

би би

бр бр      бу бу

бир бир

pine forest

бар бар

bar

риба *риба*                                                        fish

краб *краб*                                                        crab

дрова *дрова*                                              (eye)brow

бобер *бобер*                                                    beaver

брат *брат*                                                      brother

Бобер боброві брат.
A beaver is a friend for a beaver.

*Бобер боброві брат.*

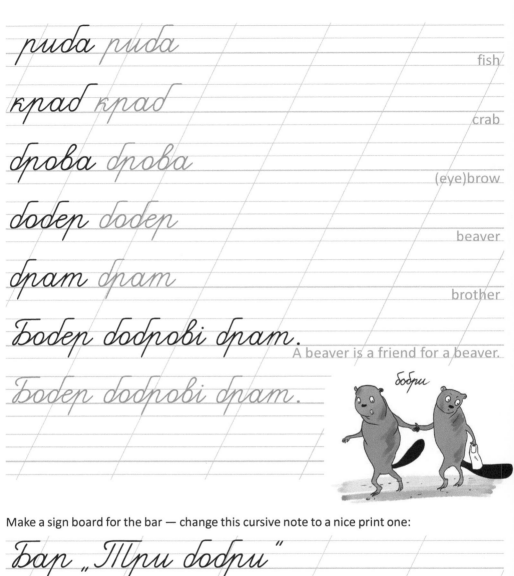
бобри

Make a sign board for the bar — change this cursive note to a nice print one:

Бар „Три бобри"
Bar "Three Beavers"

## /EN/ — LIKE N IN NO

**O Hi!!!** *Oh No!!!* **H** in Ukrainian is not pronounced as /h/ in English. It is actually that /n/ in "no".

H H

H H

*H H*

*H H*

*He He*

Not

*Ha Ha*

On

*Hi Hi*                    *HO HO*

no

*OH OH*                    *eH eH*

there

*CH CH*                    *Hm Hm*

Now you can write "no" in Ukrainian! 🎉

*Hi Hi*

*сон сон* — sleep, dream

*ніс ніс* — nose

*поні поні* — pony

*вино вино* — wine

*ранок ранок* — morning

*інтернет інтернет* — internet

Here is how you address people in Ukrainian.
Write it down in print and then cursive!

# Пане, Пані

Mr., Ms.

*пан*

*пані*

Add **не** to the model:

*не пес* ___ *кіт* ___ *банан* ___ *ранок*

# /EL/ — LIKE L IN LEMON

Different shape, same sound: Λ (or **Л** in some fonts) in Ukrainian = *L* in English.
And **лимон** = **l**emon.

Λ Λ

Λ Λ

*л л*

*л л*

*ла ла*　　　　　*лі лі*

*ле ле*　　　　　*ло ло*

*ел ел*

*ил ил*

Did you know that a stork is one of the national symbols of Ukraine?
Write "a stork" in Ukrainian:

*лелека лелека*

stork

*лелека*

*літо літо*

summer

*липа липа*

linden

*ласка ласка*

caress

*тепло тепло*

warmth

*половина половина*

half

*планета планета*

planet

*Блакитне небо, квіти, трава —*

Blue sky, flowers, grass —

*тепле літо.*

it's a warm summer.

*Блакитне небо, квіти, трава —*

*тепле літо.*

*літо*

 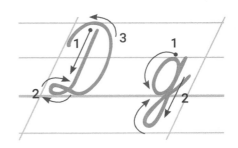

## /DE/ — LIKE D IN DOG

Ukrainian letter **Д** (another shape — **Д**) sounds similar to the English /d/. Also **Д** can be a part of the special sounds **[ДЖ]** — [d͡ʒ] and **[ДЗ]** — [d͡z] — they are pronounced quickly as one sound.

Д Д

Д Д

D D

g g

Da Da

De De

Where

gr gr                              gi gi

go go                              eg eg

godpe godpe

good (well)

Так, godpe Так, godpe

Yes, okay

37

*дар дар*

gift/

*сад сад*

garden

*дід дід*

grandfather

*доба доба*

24 hours

*дерево дерево*

tree

Find and underline **д** and **б**:

*Добрі бобри брід переброли.*

Good beavers roamed the ford.

*Добрі бобри брід переброли.*

бобри

This is **скоромовка** — a tongue twister. Try to read it as fast as you can!

# Г г

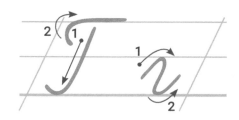

## /HE/ — CLOSE TO H IN HIKE

**Г** is our special one. It is a glottal sound which is pronounced in quite a unique way. Unlike in Russian, Bulgarian, or Serbian, **Г** in Ukrainian resembles the English sound /h/, but with more voice in it. Get some practice with the audio to this chapter!

Г Г

Г Г

Ґ Ґ

г г

Ґа Ґа

Ґр Ґр

ш ш

гі гі

го го          ге ге

The opposite of **добре** is **погано**:

*погано погано*

bad (badly)

39

гра гра
game

гори

гори гори
mountains

гірко гірко
bitterly

гарно гарно
nicely

погода погода
weather

пригоди пригоди
adventures

Is it **добре** :) or **погано** :(?

далека дорога далека дорога
a long way

тепла погода тепла погода
warm weather

багато пригод багато пригод
a lot of adventures

багато роботи багато роботи
a lot of work

40

## /U/ — LIKE OO IN POOL

Do you like буряк – *beetroot*? It is important to practice that **У** well in order to say or spell **Україна**.

У у

у у

*У у*

*У у*

*Ук Ук*

*Ур Ур*

*ун ун*          *ул ул*

*ну ну*          *ру ру*

*кут кут*

angle, corner

*гуси гуси*

geese

*угода* *угода*

agreement

*буква* *буква*

letter

**У** (with its phonetic variation — **В**) is a preposition which means "in" or "at":

*у лісі* *у лісі*

in the forest

*у полі* *у полі*

in the field

*у небі* *у небі*

in the sky

*у саду* *у саду*

in the garden

*Кіт Улас украв ковбасу у баби*

Cat Ulas stole a sausage from grandmother Ustyna.

*Устини.* *Кіт Улас украв*

*ковбасу у баби Устини.*

кіт Улас

ковбаса

# M M

## /EM/ — LIKE M IN MOM

You will like **M**. There is nothing special about it! It's like the **M** in many other languages:
**Мама** = mother, matka, madre...

**M M**

**M** M

*М М*

*м м*

*ма ма*          *мм мм*

*мо мо*          *ам ам*

*ме ме*          *ум ум*

*сім сім*

seven

*сум сум*

sadness

*море море*

sea

мак мак

poppy (plant)

мама мама

mother

мокро мокро

wet

Дмитро Дмитро

Dmytro (male name)

Марко Марко

Marko (male name)

Роман Роман

Roman (male name)

Марина Марина

Maryna (female name)

місто місто

town, city

Мілан Мілан

Milan (city)

метро метро

subway

У Марти – мак.

Martha has a poppy.

У Марти – мак.

У Марти – мак.

*Роман у метро міста Мілан.*

Roman is in the subway of Milan city.

*Роман у метро міста Мілан.*

*У Палермо метро нема.*

In Palermo, there is no subway.

*У Палермо метро нема.*

*Там – пором. Там – пором.*

There is a ferry there.

Practice writing the names of cities on the grey line. Then write down appropriate city names under each photo **in print letters.**

*Рим / Стамбул / Мадрид*

Марта is trying on skirts. Read the words in cursive and decide which skirt they indicate. Rewrite the words in **print letters.**

*міні / міді / максі*

# Ч ч

## /CHE/ — LIKE CH IN CHESS

Do you like **ch**ai? I mean **Ч**ай? Зелений **Ч**и **Ч**орний? **Чай** is any kind of tea in Ukrainian.

Ч ч

ч ч

ч ч

Ча Ча       Че Че

чі чі       ач ач

оч оч

еч еч

очі очі

eyes

час час

time

річ  річ

*thing*

човен  човен

*boat*

вечір  вечір

*evening*

початок  початок

*beginning*

чоловік  чоловік

*man*

човник  човник

*little boat*

будиночок  будиночок

*little house*

У Чака Норріса будиночок у саду.

Chuck Norris has a little house in the garden.

У Чака Норріса будиночок у саду.

будиночок у саду

Change cursive to print:

*Чилі*

Chile

*Туреччина*

Turkey

*Чорне море*

the Black Sea

Change print to cursive:

# Чад

Chad

# Мачу-Пікчу

Machu Picchu

# Словаччина

Slovakia

# Я я

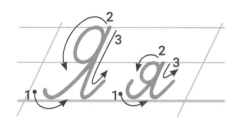

## /JA/ - LIKE YA IN YARD

Я can be pronounced in two ways depending on its position:

• **[й] + [a]** combo at the beginning of a word, after a vowel or an apostrophe sign ('). Think of the first sounds in the word *yard*. Some examples: **Я**понія — Japan, сім'**я** — family (all я's are pronounced as [йа]).

• **[a]** only after the consonants without an apostrophe sign ('). Plus, **Я** makes the consonant before softer. Like in the name Кат**я** (because of **Я**, **Т** is pronounced softly).

Я Я

Я Я

*Я Я*

*я я*

*ня ня*      *ля ля*

*яр яр*      *ея ея*

*яс яс*      *ія ія*

*яв яв*      *Яп Яп*

*Ял Ял*      *Ян Ян*

## PRONOUNCE Я AS /JA/:

• at the beginning of words • after vowels • after the apostrophe (')

*як як* — how

*ягоди ягоди* — berries

ягоди

*ідея ідея* — idea

*моя моя* — my (feminine form)

*мрія мрія* — dream

*моя мрія моя мрія* — my dream

*Японія Японія* — Japan

*Ісландія Ісландія* — Iceland

*— Яка погода? — Яка погода?* — What is the weather like?

*— Ясно. — Ясно.* — It's clear.

50

## PRONOUNCE Я AS /A/:

• after the consonants without an apostrophe sign (')

*маля маля*

baby

*земля земля*

earth, ground

*бабуся бабуся*

grandmother

*гуляти гуляти*

to walk

*дякувати дякувати*

to thank

*гусеня гусеня*

gosling

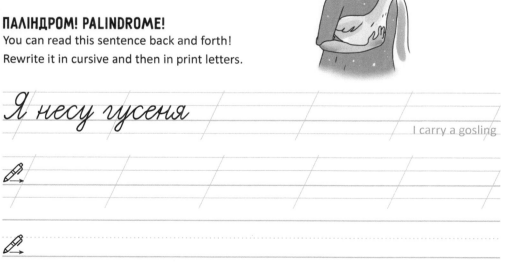

## ПАЛІНДРОМ! PALINDROME!

You can read this sentence back and forth!
Rewrite it in cursive and then in print letters.

*Я несу гусеня*

I carry a gosling

🖉

🖉

# Ю ю

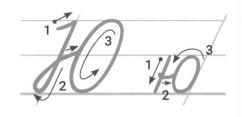

## /JU/ — LIKE YOU IN YOU

Say *you* — get **Ю**! Just like **Я**, **Ю** can be pronounced in two ways depending on its position:
- [**й**] + [**у**] combo at the beginning of a word, after a vowel or an apostrophe sign ('): **Ю**шка — soup (usually fish or mushroom soup), **Ю**пітер — Jupiter, комп'**ю**тер — computer.
- [**у**] only after the consonants without an apostrophe sign ('). Plus, **Ю** makes the consonant before softer. For example: л**ю**бов — *love* (because of **Ю**, **Л** is pronounced softly).

Ю ю

Ю ю

*Ю Ю*

*ю ю*

*Юл Юл*

*Юр Юр*

*ою ою*          *ею ею*

*сю сю*          *лю лю*

*юв юв*          *юн юн*

*Юрко Юрко* — Yurko (male name)

*Юля Юля* — Yulia (female name)

*юнак юнак* — young man

*малюнок малюнок* — drawing

*любов любов* — love

*залюбки залюбки* — pleasure

*людина людина* — person

людина

Now you can write "Thank you" in Ukrainian 🎉

*Дякую Дякую* — Thank you

✎

Now you can write "I love you!" in Ukrainian 🎉

*Я люблю тебе! — Я люблю тебе!* — Thank you

✎

– Чаю, люба? – Чаю, люба?

— Tea, darling?

– Залюбки! – Залюбки!

— With pleasure!

-ю is a common ending for the 1st person verbs. There can even be two letters **ю** at the end!

Я мию Я мию

I am washing

Я читаю Я читаю

I am reading

Я літаю Я літаю

I am flying

Я малюю Я малюю

I am drawing

Who is faster? Write down your answer:

Людина чи черепаха?

A person or a turtle?

Верблюд чи гепард?

A camel or a cheetah?

# Є є

## /JE/ — LIKE YE IN YET

Є is one of the three Ukrainian letters that can be pronounced in two ways (depending on the position):

- **[й] + [e]** combo at the beginning of a word, after a vowel or an apostrophe sign ('). Think of the first sounds in the word *yellow*. Example: єнот — a racoon.
- **[e]** only after the consonants without an apostrophe sign ('). Plus, Є makes the consonant before softer. There are not many words like these, for example: ллє — *is pouring* (because of Є, Л is pronounced softly).

Є є

є є

Є Є

є є

Єм Єм              ЄВ ЄВ

ЄН ЄН              єд єд

нє нє

єє єє

мОЄ мОЄ

my (neuter gender)

In these words **є** is pronounced as /je/:

*Єгор Єгор*

Yehor (male name)

*Євген Євген*

Yevhen (male name)

*Ємен Ємен*

Yemen

*Європа Європа*

Europe

*євро євро*

euro

*єті єті*

yeti

*єнот єнот*

raccoon

*приємно приємно*

pleasantly

And here are some words where **є** softens the previous consonant:

*синє море синє море*

blue sea

*літнє небо літнє небо*

summer sky

**Є** itself is a very useful word. It means "is" or "there is". If you want to say "there is not", use **немає**.

*Там є метро? – Є.*

Is there a subway there? – There is.

*Там є метро? – Є.*

*Там є аеропорт? – Немає.*

Is there an airport there? – There is not.

*Там є аеропорт? – Немає.*

It is very common to say **У вас є** (You have - plural or singular formal) or **У тебе є** (You have - singular informal).

*У вас є / У тебе є*

You have

*У вас є / У тебе є*

Answer the questions. Write down **є** or **немає**:

*У вас є кіт?*

Do you have a cat?

*У вас є собака?*

Do you have a dog?

*У вас є енот?*

Do you have a raccoon?

## /TSE/ — LIKE TS IN LOTS

Try to quickly say the English word *lots*, and you will get the Ukrainian **Ц** — *loTS*.

Ц ц

ц ц

Ц Ц

Цу Цу

Це Це      Цу Цу

Цм Цм      цв цв

ечу ечу      шц шц

Ця Ця

this (feminine gender)

це це

this (neuter gender)

ці ці

these (plural)

58

ціна ціна

price

цегла цегла

brick

центр центр

center

цирк цирк

circus

цукор цукор

sugar

цибуля цибуля

onion

поцілунок поцілунок

kiss

– Це цибуля?

– Is it (this) onion?

**Write in cursive and then copy in print letters:**

суниці — wild strawberries

цибуля — onion

цукор — sugar

✎ →

✎ →

**Read a little dialogue at the market:**

– Які ціни на цибулю?

What are the prices for onions?

– Які ціни на цибулю?

– Цибулі нема.

There are no onions.

– Цибулі нема.

Є суниці, полуниці.

There are wild strawberries, strawberries.

Є суниці, полуниці.

Солодкі, як цукор!

Sweet as sugar!

Солодкі, як цукор!

# З з

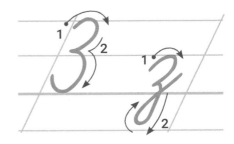

## /ZE/ — LIKE Z IN ZOO

**З** itself is easy: **З**ебра — Zebra. But what about кукуру**дз**а? **Д** and **З** together are pronounced quickly as one sound — [дз].

З з

З з

З З

з з

За За

Зі Зі

зи зи

зе зе

зр зр

ез ез

зв зв

оз оз

из из

із із

зима   зима

winter

звір   звір

wild animal

казка   казка

fairytale

козак   козак

cossack

криза   криза

crisis

зірка   зірка

star

зараз   зараз

now

пізно   пізно

late

– Звідки ти?   – Звідки ти?

Where are you from?

– З Загреба.
– From Zagreb.

– З Загреба.

Звідки ти?

Я з Загреба

Зоряна і Злата на Замбезі.

Zoriana and Zlata on the Zambezi River.

– Тут злі крокодили!

– There are angry crocodiles here!

– Тут злі крокодили!

– Звідки?   – Звідки?

– Where from?

– Не знаю, але треба

– I don't know,

забиратися, поки не

but we have to get out

пізно!

before it's too late!

– Не знаю, але треба забиратися, поки не пізно!

– Моя зачіска!

My hairstyle!

– Моя зачіска!

– Зате безпечно... – Зате безпечно...

– At least it's safe...

# ь

## /MJAKÝJ ZNAK/ — MAKES THE PREVIOUS CONSONANT SOFT

ь is a silent superhero. It does not make any sounds itself, but it changes others — it makes the sounds before it softer. We call ь **м'який знак** or **знак м'якшення** (soft sign).

ь  ь

ь  ь

Нь  Нь          нь  нь

Ть  Ть          ть  ть

Ль  Ль          ль  ль

Зь  Зь          зь  зь

Сь  Сь          сь  сь

ьо  ьо

Now you can write "Please" in Ukrainian 🎉

Будь ласка  Будь ласка

✏️

день день _день_ day

сіль сіль _сіль_ salt

кінь кінь _кінь_ horse

пальма пальма _пальма_ palm

сьогодні сьогодні _сьогодні_ today

Most of the months in Ukrainian end with **-ь**. Try to write them in cursive and print.

квітень April

вересень September

січень January

березень March

Masculine nationalities often end with **-ь**. Read the words and find out where these people come from:

○ японець *японець*

○ англієць *англієць*

○ кореєць *кореєць*

○ американець *американець*

○ австралієць *австралієць*

○ іранець *іранець*

○ італієць *італієць*

Японія 1

Англія 2

Австралія 3

Іран 4

США 5

Південна Корея 6

Італія 7

 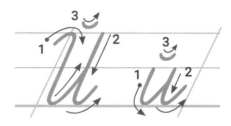

## /JOT/ — LIKE Y IN YES

**Ye**s! **Й** sounds just like the first sound in the word *yes*. By the way, this sound is part of some other Ukrainian letters: **Я** — [**йа**]; **Ю** — [**йу**]; **Є** — [**йе**]; **Ї** — [**йі**].

Й Й

й й

Й Й

й й

Йо Йо

йо йо

ій ій

ий ий

ай ай

Here is what you can shout out in Ukrainian if you are scared or surprised:

Ой! Ой!

Oh!

бульйон *бульйон*

broth

Андрій *Андрій*

Andrii (male name)

Йоко Оно *Йоко Оно*

Yoko Ono

Йоганн Себастьян Бах

Johann Sebastian Bach

*Йоганн Себастьян Бах*

**-ий** is a common ending which identifies a masculine adjective or pronoun.
Find such words below and underline them.

– Ну, який той каньйон?

– Well, what kind of canyon is that?

*– Ну, який той каньйон?*

– Великий... Глибокий...

–Big... Deep...

*– Великий... Глибокий...*

великий каньйон

68

**Колір** is a color. **Білий колір** – white color. One common color ends with **-ій** – find out which one below!

*зелений* green

*червоний* red

*синій* dark blue

*блакитний* blue

*білий* white

*чорний* black

*коричневий* brown

*помаранчевий* orange

**Марта** has dyed her hair four times. Write down which colors she has chosen.

# X x

## /КНА/ — LIKE WH IN WHO

**X**то це? *WHo* is this? This is **X** — Ukrainian /h/. For example, the verb ра**ху**вати (to count) has *who* in it. Unlike **Г**, letter **X** is a voiceless sound, it is very quiet.

X X

X X

𝒳 𝒳

𝓍 𝓍

𝒳о 𝒳о

𝒳е 𝒳е

𝓍і 𝓍і          𝓍р 𝓍р

𝓍л 𝓍л          𝓍м 𝓍м

і𝓍 і𝓍          а𝓍 а𝓍

Are you in the mood for a laugh? These words imitate laughing in Ukrainian:

𝒳а–ха! 𝒳а–ха!

Ha-ha!

70

хата хата

house

халепа халепа

trouble

хімія хімія

chemistry

хлопчик хлопчик

little boy

хмара хмара

cloud

хвилина хвилина

minute

Let's practice writing the names of some Ukrainian cities. Can you find them on the map online?

Хуст Хуст

Хотин Хотин

Херсон Херсон

Харків Харків

Хмельницький Хмельницький

*Хто? Хто?*

Who?

**Check out these Ukrainian proverbs and idioms with хто:**

*Хто в ліс, хто по дрова.*

Some go to the woods, some go to get firewood.
(about people doing different things when they are supposed to do the same).

*Хто в ліс, хто по дрова.*

**Let's switch to the love wave. Underline x in these proverbs:**

*Хто як постеле, так і виспиться.*

How one makes their bed, one will sleep (actions have consequences).

*Хто як постеле, так і виспиться.*

*Хоч ох, та вдвох. Хоч ох, та вдвох.*

Even in despair we are together.

*Хоч лайся, та не цурайся.*

You can fight with me but don't ignore me.

*Хоч лайся, та не цурайся.*

72

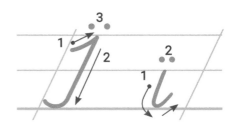

## /JI/ — LIKE YIE IN YIELD

Ї is a cute letter that is always pronounced as two sounds: **[й] + [і].** It sounds similar to the beginning of the word *yeast* in English.

Ї Ї

Ї Ї

ї ї

ї ї

їн їн    їв їв

їл їл    їз їз

еї еї    аї аї

ої ої    ії ії

мої мої

my (plural)

твої твої

your (plural)

*їм їм*

I'm eating

*їду їду*

I'm going (by transport)

*краї краї*

lands; edges

*країна країна*

country

Now you can write Ukraine 🎉

# Україна

*Україна Україна*

Ukraine

And the name of our capital 🎉

# Київ

*Київ Київ*

Kyiv

Nouns ending with **-я** change to **-ї** when we talk about locations. Follow the example:

*Англія — в Англії*

England — in England

*Японія — у Японі___*

Japan — in Japan

*Австралія — в _____*

Australia — in Australia

74

## /SHA/ — LIKE SH IN SHORT

Ш = /sh/. In Ukrainian, there are plenty of words that come from English. Like **шорти** — *shorts*.

Ш Ш

Ш Ш

Ш Ш

ш ш

Шв Шв

Шр Шр

ша ша          шу шу

шш шш          ші ші

шш шш          аш аш

шл шл          шк шк

шум шум

noise

тиша тиша

silence

шахи шахи

chess

шість шість

six

швидко швидко

fast

шоколад шоколад

chocolate

шкарпетки шкарпетки

socks

шкарпетки

Швеція Швеція

Sweden

Швейцарія Швейцарія

Switzerland

Шрі-Ланка Шрі-Ланка

Sri Lanka

Їде миша долиною

The mouse is going through the valley

Морквяною машиною.

By a carrot car.

Поки в місто доповзе,

While crawling into the city,

Всю машину погризе.

It will bite the whole car.

Іван Малкович

Ivan Malkovych

**Now write this poem in cursive yourself:**

Їде миша долиною

Морквяною машиною.

Поки в місто доповзе,

Всю машину погризе.

Іван Малкович

## /SHCHA/ — LIKE SHCH IN FRESH CHERRIES

Щ is a combo letter that includes two distinct sounds: **Ш + Ч = Щ**. You can try to pronounce it by saying *freSH CHerries* = SH + CH = **Щ**.

Щ Щ
Щ Щ

Щ Щ

Щ Щ

Ща Ща                     Ще Ще

щи щи                     щу щу

рщ рщ

Що? Що?
What?

що що
what, that

ще ще
still, yet, more

дощ дощ

rain

борщ борщ

borsch

щиро щиро

sincerely

щастя щастя

happiness

прізвище прізвище

last name

дощ

Скоромовка!

Tongue twister!

Бабин біб розцвів у дощ,

Grandma's beans blossomed in the rain,

Буде бабі дід у борщ.

There will be beans for grandma in borscht.

Бабин біб розцвів у дощ,

Буде бабі дід у борщ.

79

# Ж ж

 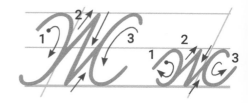

## /ZHE/ — LIKE S IN VISION

The fancy letter **Ж** makes **/ʒ/** sound as in the English words trea/ʒ/ure, u/ʒ/ual, /ʒ/enre. Also, **ж** is a part of the complex sound **[дж]** which is pronounced fast (like in *J-eans* — **дж**инси).

Ж Ж

Ж Ж

Ж Ж

ж ж

Жа Жа

Же Же

жо жо

жу жу

жв жв

жл жл

iж iж

вж вж

вже вже

already

*їжа* *їжа* food

*їжак* *їжак* hedgehog

*жаба* *жаба* frog

*жарт* *жарт* joke

*жінка* *жінка* woman

*жовтий* *жовтий* yellow

*жовтень* *жовтень* October

*Женева* *Женева* Geneva

*жук* *жук* bug

**Дж** is usually pronounced as one sound — /d͡ʒ/ — like j in jam.

*бджоли* *бджоли*

*джем* *джем*

бджоли

джем

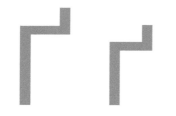
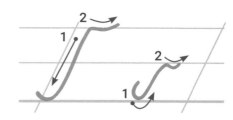

## /GE/ — LIKE G IN GO

ґ is a unique letter, only used in the Ukrainian alphabet. And for this reason... it was banned and forbidden to use during the Soviet times. Poor ґ! As a result, ґ came back to independent Ukraine in way fewer words than before. Now it is only used in about 30 common words and in some dialects. ґ is very easy to pronounce: it's the /g/ in *go*.

head bump

crow

*ґанок* *ґанок*

porch

*ґудзик* *ґудзик*

button

*ґвалт* *ґвалт*

rumpus

*ґедзь* *ґедзь*

horse-fly

*ґазда* *ґазда*

master of the house

*ґрати* *ґрати*

bars

*ґрунт* *ґрунт*

soil

*Який ґедзь тебе вкусив?*

Which horse-fly stung you? (Why are you behaving like this?)

*Який ґедзь тебе вкусив?*

*ґедзь*

83

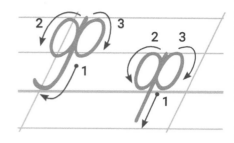

## /EF/ — LIKE F IN FAT

The letter **Ф** is relatively newer to the alphabet, it appears only in foreign words. That is why it is easy to pronounce: it is **F** in *proFession* — професія or *Film* — фільм.

Ф Ф

ф ф

ф ф

ф ф

Фе Фе       Фр Фр

фі фі       фа фа

фл фл

фо фо

Change print to cursive:

# Фейсбук

*Facebook*

84

фото фото

фах фах

profession

Софія Софія

Sofia (female name)

ферма ферма

farm

фарба фарба

paint

фарба

флешка флешка

flash drive

фігура фігура

figure

фіранка фіранка

curtain

Федір Федір

Fedir (male name)

Франція Франція

France

Франкфурт Франкфурт

Frankfurt

**Апостроф** — an apostrophe is a special symbol. It is used before **я, ю, є, ї** (when they are pronounced as two sounds: /ja/, /ju/, /je/, /ji/) — typically after **б, п, ф, м, ф** or other consonants.

п'ять  п'ять

five

м'яз  м'яз

muscle

сузір'я  сузір'я

constellation

комп'ютер  комп'ютер

computer

б'ю  б'ю

I beat

п'є  п'є

he / she / it drinks

з'єднати  з'єднати

to join

з'їсти  з'їсти

to eat up

під'їзд  під'їзд

stairwell, entrance

# Місце для практики

# Відповіді

**page 15**

Оксана, Аля і Соломія у школі іноземних мов.

**page 17**

Колискова

Котику сіренький, котику біленький,

Котку волохатий, не ходи по хаті.

**page 22**

е. Коротко

е. Ракета

**page 24**

рок ②     Поттер ③     парк ①

е. рок     Поттер     парк

**page 28**

кит — кити

карта — карти

парк — парки

паспорт — паспорти

ракета — ракети

кит     кіт

**page 32**

Бар "Три бобри"

**page 34**

✐ Пане, Пані

✐ Пане, Пані

не кіт    не банан    не ранок

**page 38**

Добрі бобри брід перебрели.

**page 45**

✐ Рим    Стамбул    Мадрид

✐ максі

✐ міні

✐ міді

**page 48**

✐ Чилі

✐ Туреччина

✐ Чорне море

✐ Чад

✐ Мачу-Пікчу

✐ Словаччина

**page 51**

✐ Я несу гусеня

**page 54**

Людина

Гепард

**page 59**

✐ суниці    цибуля    цукор

## page 65

л. квітень

л. вересень

л. січень

л. березень

## page 66

1) японець

2) англієць

6) кореєць

5) американець

3) австралієць

4) іранець

7) італієць

## page 68

Який, Великий, Глибокий

## page 69

л. синій   зелений   помаранчевий   червоний

## page 72

Хто як постеле, так і виспиться.

Хоч ох, та вдвох.

Хоч лайся, та не цурайся.

## page 74

Японія — у Японії

Австралія — в **Австралії**

## page 84

л. Фейсбук

# Про авторок

## Наталія Пендюр

Natalia Pendiur was born in Kyiv and studied at the Institute of Journalism at Taras Shevchenko University and Slavic Studies at the Masaryk University in Czechia.

Natalia has many hobbies and professions — among others, she is a Ukrainian teacher, writer, artist, and illustrator. Having such various skills, Natalia collaborated with Ukrainian Lessons to create the Easy Ukrainian Book: Як іноземці козака рятували (2021) — a fascinating story in simplified Ukrainian with exercises and Natalia's hand-drawn illustrations.

When her student in Czechia asked her to teach her Ukrainian handwriting, Natalia was puzzled at first. But giving it some thought, she developed a progressive system of teaching Cyrillic letters one by one — by incorporating the letters learned into the examples for the next letter.

Just like with her Easy Ukrainian Book, Natalia created all the illustrations for this workbook by herself — this time in color.

*Анна Огойко*

Anna Ohoiko is a Ukrainian language specialist, teacher, and founder of UkrainianLessons.com. She is originally from the town of Polonne in Khmelnytska oblast, in central-western Ukraine.

Having always been passionate about languages, Anna graduated from Kyiv-Mohyla Academy and got a Master's degree in Theory, History of Ukrainian Language and Comparative Studies.

From 2017 to 2018, she taught Ukrainian at the University of Pennsylvania through the Fulbright program. As of 2022, she works from her home office in Sweden, bringing inspiring resources for learning Ukrainian out there to the world.

Anna led the production of this book, wrote pronunciation intros and recorded the audio.

# Про Ukrainian Lessons

This workbook was created by **UkrainianLessons.com** — a cozy educational platform that provides good-quality modern materials for learning Ukrainian. It was founded by **Anna Ohoiko** shortly after the Ukrainian Revolution of Dignity in 2014. Since then, the UL team has been providing various materials and support for Ukrainian learners with blog posts, books, videos, infographics, and their structured podcast courses — **Ukrainian Lessons Podcast** and **5 Minute Ukrainian**.

We are also proud to host the most active **Ukrainian learners community on Facebook** — a group where everyone can ask questions, practice Ukrainian and share their favorite materials. You can join this friendly community at: **ukrainianlessons.com/fbgroup**.

" *I am so happy to have stumbled upon this site/podcast! It is wonderful that the Ukrainian Lessons Podcast is working to address that inaccessibility by providing the free podcast & an abundance of resources to further our language and cultural learning.*

Lilly F from the United States

" *I think the Ukrainian language is the most beautiful of all the Slavic languages due to its musicality and rhythm... I feel lucky to come across Anna's way of teaching it! It is friendly and very well focused on securing the steps one by one as I am progressing through the entire course. And the best part is that it doesn't stop at the basics... It gets gradually more difficult as you go... Lovely! I would recommend everyone to subscribe to the premium membership. It justifies its value 100%... better when you leave your українські friends amazed by your progress in their beautiful language.*

Luis A. Zapata from Peru

" *On my first visit to Kyiv, I felt confident in my already obtained basic skills in Ukrainian and was even slightly complimented in a souvenir shop. I owe a good deal a huge credit to ukrainianlessons.com and Anna. She takes you into this language, gradually enhancing new words and grammar.*

Wilhelm Fuchs from Germany

" *You can find it all here in a most palatable and well-prepared mix — grammar, vocabulary, pronunciation, language functions — all served up engagingly with a serving of cultural knowledge topping it up like a spoonful of сметана! It doesn't get any better than this!*

Христина Сікорська from Winnipeg, Canada

### Easy Ukrainian Book (intermediate & advanced level)

If you already have some progress in Ukrainian and are looking for an immersive experience, check out this book. It is an easy read with exercises, vocabulary lists and audio. Its fun story is about Beatrice from Spain and Brian from the USA who are going to have an unforgettable summer in Ukraine… Available as paperback or ebook — whichever format you choose, you get free audio!

Find out more at **ukrainianlessons.com/cossack**

### Ukrainian Phrasebook For Helping Refugees

Since the beginning of the brutal Russian invasion of Ukraine in 2022, people around the world #StandWithUkraine and put enormous effort into supporting the refugees. This phrasebook is for everyone helping Ukrainian people — at the borders, at immigration centers, at humanitarian organizations, in their homes, or at a distance. It includes 20 practical chapters of the most important Ukrainian words and phrases to facilitate communication and demonstrate care. Additional links to expand certain topics make this book an excellent basis for further Ukrainian learning.

Find out more at **ukrainianlessons.com/phrasebook**

## Ukrainian Lessons Podcast

Are you looking for a well-structured and easily accessible Ukrainian language course that can easily fit into your life? Ukrainian Lessons Podcast is exactly what its name says: Lessons of Ukrainian in the format of a podcast. This means you can enjoy learning Ukrainian with a real teacher from the comfort of your car, on your morning jog, or while cooking. Give it a go — all the lessons are free — and if you enjoy it and want to dig deeper, subscribe to the premium membership to receive PDF lesson notes and digital flashcards.

Find out more at **ukrainianlessons.com/thepodcast** or look for Ukrainian Lessons Podcast in your podcast app.

## 5 Minute Ukrainian

This series of mini-lessons is all about conversations. Each episode of 5 Minute Ukrainian contains a short dialogue that you will listen to at a natural and slow speed. Then your host Anna will teach you some essential phrases for that particular situation. Apart from the dialogues, there are also useful vocabulary boosters and grammar point episodes. You can also subscribe to receive comprehensive lesson notes with exercises and flashcards.

Find out more at **ukrainianlessons.com/fmu** or look for 5 Minute Ukrainian in your podcast app.